THE DIGITISATION PLAYBOOK

A SIMPLE GUIDE TO TRANSFORM YOUR MICROBUSINESS

VINUSHA NARAPAREDDY &
ANYA PALLAMREDDY

This book is dedicated to all the businesses that became extinct during the Coronavirus Disease (COVID-19) Pandemic. India lost hundreds. Each and every one had a unique and powerful story to tell.

Contents

Foreword

There can't be a better fortune than writing a foreword for a book written by two teenage authors. They will write many books in their lives and with this first book of theirs, I will forever become a part of a great story of the future world, when I won't be around.

What would the future world be like? Let us say, in 2025. Population 10 billion, ruled by a Technology Singularity, where everybody is coded, indexed, tracked, and operating in a Matrix. There would be matrices within matrices but all following mathematical rules.

We have already seen how online delivery of goods, food, and medicines have increased quality, efficiency, and convenience for everyone, besides generating huge employment for young people, and of course, profit for large corporations.

A silent digital revolution is on the roll. New generations of vendors are getting linked to global supply chains using technology. Features like Barcodes, QR codes and RF IDs are everywhere and are indeed a part of our lives. You can buy one banana, or drink coconut water from a street vendor, and pay by your phone.

This book is straight and lean, written in a clear manner and both transparent and unpretentious about what it says. The success stories are authentic and taletelling. Resources are cited and the intellectual integrity of the authors shines through every page of the book.

I look at microbusinesses as buds that would blossom tomorrow if protected well. They essentially represent unique ideas and skills of entrepreneurs, which would not come from big businesses. These are also a testimony to the spirit of entrepreneurship and risk-taking ability of common people. So, it is logical that they should be provided business assistance and small amounts of credit to support them by the larger corporations and government organizations, without strings attached.

I see The Digitisation Playbook by Anya and Vinusha as a trumpet announcing the beginning of a new era of One World-One System and place it by the side of Small Is Beautiful: A Study of Economics As If People Mattered by E. F. Schumacher, published in 1973. This book is going to trigger a runaway reaction of self-improvement cycles in the New World.

• • •

Arun Tiwari
Hyderabad
July 2021

Preface

Microbusinesses, especially in a country like India, are an important part of our community. Besides making customized products and sharing a unique relationship with customers unlike most other forms of businesses, microbusinesses form the basis of our economy and everyday-life, providing essential services without which we couldn't survive.

Being business enthusiasts we, Anya and Vinusha, were especially disheartened to see many microbusinesses (most with so much potential to grow) shutting down due to the brutal COVID-19 pandemic. About ten to eleven local businesses were forced to close in our own neighborhoods itself for a range of reasons: lack of access to financial resources, decline in consumer demand, inability to adhere to expensive health and safety regulations. However, after conversing with many microbusiness owners, we came to understand that they were especially struggling to adapt to the changing consumer trends in a digital economy. Thinking about the scale of the situation, in a country with millions of people, we were inspired to do something to help microbusiness owners keep their ideas and livelihoods alive.

With this guide, a somewhat "step-by-step how to" resource, we hope to help struggling business owners adapt to the new reality we are living in. With the world becoming a contactless one and consumers preferring to shift to the online space, many small businesses (without access to the right resources) can find it hard and to make a smooth transition to the digital environment. As our first step, we tried to break down this seemingly difficult process of digitisation and provide a starting point for business owners like you. Microbusinesses are the backbone of our society and with planned organization and successful execution, you will soon be able to turn your enterprise into a success story.

We hope you take away from this guide useful information but also creativity as there is no one way to go about digitizing your business. Have fun with it, just as we had writing this book, and good luck!

Anya Pallamreddy and Vinusha Narapareddy.

CHAPTER I

Section 1: Introduction

Let us begin by understanding what microbusinesses are and what it means to digitise them. A microbusiness, also known as a micro-enterprise, is a business earning less than 1 crore in income. It usually operates with fewer than ten people. They grow with the help of start-up loans or "microcredit", a type of credit provided by banks to people who have no credit (does not depend on your past debts etc.) or employment history.

Now that we have understood what a microbusiness is, we will explain what digitisation means. Digitisation is the automation of existing operations such as documentation, payments and advertising. For example, instead of keeping physical records of your invoices, using online applications to store this information will improve the efficiency of your business and save time.

Digitisation is becoming increasingly important, especially given the current times with the COVID-19 pandemic. With lockdowns and quarantine, our economy is moving to a more contactless space and businesses that cannot adapt to this will not be able to survive. Digitisation has become an everyday necessity. Another reason business owners, like you, should consider digitising your business is that you will receive multiple benefits like reduced costs, increased security, improved productivity all while increasing customer satisfaction and convenience. With a growing number of smartphone users today's consumers prefer to use online platforms.

Many business owners are reluctant to digitise their business in the fear of how complicated it seems, but this is a myth. There are many free resources (websites, applications and this book!) that are extremely easy to use and accessible to all types of businesses, all on your mobile phone.

Still not convinced? Well these facts might do the job.

> A survey by Google-Kantar found that 79% of small businesses had expressed interest in learning about digitisation. This should encourage you to start as well.

> India has more than half a billion internet users: that is 500000000 people! Be where your consumers are.

> Studies have also shown that companies that moved to virtual operations have lowered their costs by almost 36% on average. Lower costs mean higher profits.

> As per statistical data, the number of online shoppers is rapidly growing and predicted to reach 220,000,000 (220 million) by 2025. As a result of this, all the operations need to happen online.

Though all this might seem like doing the impossible, we assure you it is not hard. Do not worry, we have put together a list of general tips, useful resources, and cost-friendly advice to help you start digitising your business today!

CHAPTER II

Section 2: Planning Ahead

Now that you have a basic understanding of what this book will cover. Let us think about how you can start planning and preparing your business for this transition.

- **Start slow, make sure you are comfortable**

We will be mentioning a number of resources in this guide, but it is important to start slow, take your time and work at your own pace. Build a strong foundation.

- **Focus on your needs, essentials first**

We have organised resources in the order of importance (as we felt). However, depending on your business and what you, as an entrepreneur, are comfortable with; feel free to skip over some. Every business is different and there is NO RIGHT order. For example, a boutique might need to focus on social media marketing (do not worry we will explain what it is), while a bakery might want to focus on digital payments. Digitisation is not something you can do in one day; it will take time and it is important to focus on what your business needs **right now**.

- **Plan ahead**

Digitising is a step by step process, so set a timeline and plan before you start. Without a plan, you will end up wasting time and resources. First, understand the resources that you can use and plan a budget. You can always change your timeline but try not to.

- **Inform your employees, make sure they are comfortable**

Meet with your employees and share your plans with them. Take their feedback, listen to any worries they might have and ask what they might be expecting. They might be a little hesitant at first but explain to them that even with virtual operations their work is equally important. Remember that your employees must also get used to the changes. The key is to build a strong and well-supported foundation.

- **Inform your customers**

This is a later step, but make sure your customers are comfortable with the new changes. Be ready to answer any questions they might have, so make sure you understand them well before letting your customers know.

To end here are a few resources that will help you throughout your digitisation journey. To access any resource in this book, simply type the name into the google app on your phone or www.google.comwebsite. Some of these resources are also available as applications on the AppStore and Google Play Store.

>Google Account- Most resources that we mention in this book require a google account to sign up, so we suggest you make an account first. Simply type "how to make a google account" on Google to get started.

> EverNoteis a free app that can be used for note-taking, planning, organising tasks, and saving data or records.

> *Useful Tip*: You can now use Google in different languages. Type google.com/preferences#languagesin Google to change to your preferred language.

Do you not understand something? Here are three ways that will help:-

> Go to Google and type "how to" + the sentence you do not understand or "meaning of" + the word you do not understand.

> In case you are using a website that is in a language you do not understand, type "google translate to" + the language you are most comfortable with. This will help translate the sentence to your language.

> You can also contact customer service on any of the websites: there are people available who speak many languages. They will assist you and answer all your questions.

Keep these tips in mind as you read the guide and remember, **go slow**.

CHAPTER III

Section 3: Finance

What is Finance?

Finance is a broad term for all things money. Whether it is making payments, borrowing from the bank or managing accounts, all these processes come under finance. Without proper financial planning many micro businesses cannot survive. Digitising this segment of your business will make it a lot easier to plan ahead and use your data to predict future costs.

- Let us start with the most basic requirement:**Funding (Money or Capital for the business to digitise and grow)**

All businesses need funding to grow, and it is easier for larger, well established businesses to get access to funding. This is because they have a credit history (information about past debts and how long one takes to pay back loans) and collateral (an asset or property which the bank can take away in case the borrower cannot pay back the loan - it is a safety net or guarantee for the bank). However, microbusinesses cannot afford to have collateral and usually do not have credit history either; this is why you as a microbusiness owner should know all the available channels to get funding.

Below are a few suggestions:-

> A good place to start will be looking at what the government schemes have to offer (see Section 9 Government Schemes for Microbusinesses). For example,

businesses with manufacturing activity like retail trade, educational institutions can get funded (loans without collateral) through the Credit Guarantee Fund Scheme. If your business is in the service sector, it is also eligible for funding under this loan plan.

> There are some institutions called Microfinance banks that provide loans to microbusinesses in India. Micro Financing Institutions (MFI) provide microloans (loans less than 1 lakh without collateral) and microinsurance (to protect microbusinesses from uncertainties like the COVID-19 pandemic in exchange for small regular payments also known as premiums). Microloans tend to have high interest rates. There are many MFIs in India such as Annapurna Microfinance and Equitas Microfinance.

> Crowdfunding is the process of raising small amounts from a large number of people. It involves simply posting a video explaining your product or business and if people like it, they will fund it. All for free. A popular crowdfunding resource is kickstarter.com (> "start a project").

• **Setting up a bank account**

To make use of the resources mentioned in this section; it is easier to set up a bank account first. Microbusinesses can make use of their existing bank accounts and link them to resources or set up a new "current account" for operating their businesses. razorpay.com/x/current-accounts offers current account services.

• **Digitizing Transactions**

This is probably the easiest way to digitise your business. Digitizing payments would mean moving away from cash and accepting other forms of payments such as scan to pay. Here are some reasons why this can be a beneficial change:-

> With an increased number of customers (online and offline), digital payments are the future of a contactless economy.

> It is cheap because card payments charge per transaction and the costs can be high.

> Digital payments in India are predicted to grow to 72% of all payment transactions by 2025, so adapt before it is too late!

> Safer in terms of financial security and more convenient as you do not need to keep track of everyday transactions - this will save a lot of time. This will eliminate accounting errors and you can easily get an accurate record of all your transactions at the end of the day.

> You can maintain a smoother cash flow (no need to deposit money into your account because online payments go directly to your bank account and you can directly make rent and other payments through this platform and there is no need to take out money to pay vendors).

> Since this process is much easier than paying through cash, customers are more likely to buy faster and not think twice about it (called impulse buying). Instant payment and customers will not have constraints of time or location.

Resources for creating means of digital payments:-

>business.paytm.com> "become a paytm merchant" > "create an account". Download the paytm application on your mobile and follow the instructions. Paytm also provides other banking resources such as a savings account.

> Pay.google.com Google Pay for Business is a simple and secure digital payment service made for all types of businesses. You can receive instant payments directly to

your bank account, and it allows new customers to learn about your business. You can use the app in English, Hindi, Bengali, Gujarati, Kannada, Marathi, Tamil, or Telugu.

- **Organising your financial data and preparing balance sheets and other statements**

It is important to digitise your accounting process as it is a more reliable form of storing and analysing your data to predict future costs and profits. Everything from preparing your profit-loss statement (a document with all your costs and earnings) and filing taxes can be done using quickbooks.intuit.com/in.They offer a free trial for 30 days and charge just Rs. 529 per month after you sign up.

Useful tip: If you are a very small business then Google Sheets **(see Section 4 Organising Data)**is useful for adding data in a tabular form (columns and rows).

Finance is the backbone of every business. If you are starting or expanding your business to the online space, you need to obtain capital or money. Carefully consider the type of finance and the methods of sourcing it, as this could later affect how you run your business.

CHAPTER IV

Section 4: Organising Data

If you're looking to grow your microbusiness, it is important to get started the right way! To achieve your business growth in the next few years, it is essential to make sure your operations and data are organised. While this might be easier for large businesses that have access to more resources, it is not impossible to arrange your data efficiently. How can you do this when you are tight on cash or only have a few employees? Keep reading to understand.

• **Identify the objectives of your microbusiness**

Firstly, the purpose of your data should influence how you manage your data. If it doesn't, you could waste a lot of time and costs analyzing the wrong kind of data and collecting the wrong kinds of resources. Try to ask yourself and your employees questions like "what are the goals of my business?", "what data do I need to meet these goals?" and "what type of insights and information do I need to be able to meet my objectives?" If you consistently prioritise these ideas, you will successfully be able to determine processes, tools and more.

• **Manage your storage and establish how exactly you will handle your data**

To handle data effectively, you need to have concrete ways to collect, store, and prepare it for further analysis. Analysis will be useful when making business decisions for the future. Here are some general steps that can be applied when gathering and evaluating data:-

> Look at all the data sources that you think you want to use. Do you have enough data or do you need additional data? How will you collect new data? Consider the tools you're already using to manage data.

> Consider resources that are already available to store data. At the same time, start to prepare your data for any type of analysis that you might need it for. How will you transform any basic data to process it? Try to consider different resources to collect data, while also ensuring your data is safe and cannot get lost.

> *Useful tip*: Use infogram.com/appto graph your data visually and find trends in your data. This tool is a little complex to use, but you can always try because it can prove to be very useful!

> How will you store data? How will you keep it secure? Which teams will control which parts of the data? How will you communicate data insights? Find a way to run the data analysis and get appropriate insights. For example, if you find a trend in your data that 75% of people who click on a certain brand of a fridge always immediately click away to another, then you know that in your upcoming sales you should be pushing for the second brand.

> *Useful tip*: Always make a copy of your data before using it to test new resources: this way you won't lose it by mistake. Once you have processed your data, make sure to delete the backup as it can get confusing to have multiple copies of the same data (see subpoint Google Drive in this Section).

- **Eliminate unnecessary storage - focus on what is needed**

It is no longer efficient to create multiple backups of everything which is both costly and a waste of time.

Instead, your business needs to manage its data efficiently and intelligently. You need to understand what your business has and how it's used, and protect and manage it well. Digital business transformation offers an opportunity to manage your information more effectively and avoid the problems that come from storing large amounts of unnecessary data.

- **Use Google Drive**

Cloud-based resources are extremely useful in our opinion, as they enable you to automatically store important documents of all types (Google documents, Google sheets for financial accounts, Google slides for presentations, and Google forms) and also automatically store edit history. In other words, the drive enables you to edit, store, and collaborate on documents, whether you work alone or in a team. The best part, however? It is free (unless you want to store beyond 15 GB of data of course). In case you lose your phone and don't have paper copies, you can always use the drive to retain your data. To access your Google Drive go to drive.google.com/drive and sign up.

- **Data Security**

One of the most overlooked elements to a digital transformation is security. Cybercrime is a massive threat: you have to protect your data. It can be corrupted, stolen, held hostage and mismanaging its security can cause a lot of problems. For example, use nordpass.com to manage your passwords (this resource offers a free 1 user plan). This program stores your passwords together in the mobile and desktop app. This can automatically be done in a browser like Google Chrome.

- **Communications**

As we've mentioned before, make sure your employees and customers are on the same page as you. In terms of communicating with your employees, one good way to keep in touch regularly is by holding short but effective online meetings. This could be done over a range of platforms, though personally we highly recommend Google Meets (meet.google.com). This feature comes in handy as and when you create a Google account, and is easily accessible. Google Calendar is also really efficient for recording meetings and other important dates automatically and accordingly sending you updates and reminders. Holding conversations with your employees online as well as using the calendar feature to remind yourself of important events perhaps associated with your customers can be super beneficial to your microbusiness.

- **Maintain a standard way to name and organise files**

Regardless of where the data is being stored – on a desktop, cloud drive, or in a specific software platform – you should have a hierarchy of folders to neatly organise files. Naming files and folders correctly is extremely important. There should be a documented method of naming files and once you choose a particular method, it must be strictly followed. A failure to follow the right naming method allows files to be easily lost (a useful naming method is consistent, meaningful, and allows data to be found easily). Archive and delete files that are no longer necessary, and you'll make things easier on your team.

Other resources that have proven to be extremely useful:

> **Evernote**: this is extremely useful to create to-do items, find ideas, make contract information, etc. This app is also really beneficial to create quick, efficient notes at any time anywhere. This app can also sync all of your notes and lists to all your devices automatically. Above all it ensures you stay organised and hassle-free!

It is important to, if you haven't already, get involved in the managing, storing, securing and utilizing of the data that you are able to collect. It is a crucial step to digitising your business.

CHAPTER V

Section 5: Advertising

What is Marketing?

Marketing is the process of spreading awareness about your business, brand, products and services. It is important because even if your business has a good product, customers will not buy it unless they know about it. There are ways of marketing offline, but digital marketing has growing opportunities and we will discuss them in this section.

Here are different forms of digital marketing:-

- **Website**

A website is a web page that can be designed by you or your employees and often has details about your products and your brand. Customers can access the website using a link. For example www.google.com is a website. It is important to create a website because it boosts brand image and provides all the information about your business in one location, including contact details. Remember to keep your website name simple, so customers can access it easily.

To make your own website here are the free resources through which you can easily set up your website:-

> <u>Wix.com</u>
> <u>WordPress.com</u>
> <u>Google Business</u>

Useful tip: When creating a website use and include bright colours, pictures, customer feedback, products and pricing if you wish and contact details (email id, phone number). Try to add hyperlinks (highlight, right click and "link") so users can find related information easily. Testimonials, too, can be a great way to give your business the right edge over others. Whether it's via Google, TrustPilot or for a dedicated testimonials section on your website, people trust other people. You'll have to ask your customers for these, as people don't very often give them naturally. Just a gentle prompt will do the trick!

- **Email Marketing**

As the name suggests, email marketing is advertising by sending out emails. Email marketing involves creating a poster and sending it out to your customer's emails. It is important to not overdo it and spam your customers. Email marketing is useful when informing your customers about promotions, new products or services.

A good place to start with email marketing is by using this free resource:-

Mailchimp.com

Useful tips: There are different ways to create a business email list. A good place to start is by asking your existing customers to fill a form with their email addresses or requesting new customers for their email when they make a purchase. Also try to include the customer's name in the email if you can as this adds a personal touch!

- **Google Advertisements**

Google offers paid advertisements which can appear in search results in Google or through Google ads that appear on other everyday websites. In fact, Google will also pay you to feature other company ads on your business website (see Google Adsense Program if you are interested in earning extra money-google.com/adsense/start).

Another option is to create a free Google Business account (Go to business.google.com/create> click on "Get started") that will help you in creating a free account and represent your business online. You can even create a free website on this platform by clicking on the "Website Menu." Creating a Google business account allows your business to be listed on Google Maps, the local section of Google Search, and the right-side panel of the google search page. This panel appears on the right side of your screen basically provides an entire overview and profile of what you might be looking for.

- **Online business directories**

An online business directory is a listing place for websites. Any type of website could be listed in an online directory. Some online directories are huge and cover every topic that someone could create a website for, while others are very small and specific to a niche. This means that online directories will direct you to just about any website that you want to find. All you have to do is perform a search in the online directory for a specific topic, or browse through the various categories until you find the type of websites you are looking for. A classic example of a popular online directory is YellowPages.inor (organised by business type) in which advertising is sold.

- **Social Media Marketing**

This refers to marketing done through social media applications such as Facebook, Instagram and Twitter.

17

Since there is a lot of information about social media marketing, we decided to cover it in another section of this guide **(see Section 6 Social Media Marketing).**

CHAPTER VI

Section 6: Social Media Marketing

What is Social Media Marketing?

Social Media Marketing is a type of marketing that is done using popular social media applications such as Facebook and Instagram. This form of marketing includes many different ways including paid advertising, direct messaging, posts and stories.

Why is Social Media Marketing useful?

Although Social Media Marketing may not seem ideal for every business, it is actually one of the easiest and fastest ways to reach out to your existing and new customers. It requires regularly updating your platforms, but it is definitely worth your time. Here are some reasons that will convince you to create your business account today.

> It is very cost-effective (even free if you choose) and easy to market on social media platforms. You also have more control over the content you share.

> It builds brand image, awareness and customer loyalty

> You can use these platforms to interact with your consumers in real-time and understand their needs by looking at past data on the account (we will discuss this in detail later)

> By spending only a few hours per week, over 91% of marketers said that social marketing increased awareness about their brand and improved user experience.

> If you are a local business, **targeted ads**based on a user's location will cut down costs significantly.

> If your competitors are using this form of advertising and you don't, it will give your competitors an advantage over your business.

- **Visual Resources and Tools**

One of the keys to social media posting is high-quality images. However, finding copyright-free images can be difficult in case you cannot afford to pay for images. Here are a few websites that offer high-resolution images for free:-

> unsplash.com

> pixabay.com

> burst.shopify.com

Useful tip: Remember to choose images that are of the right size for posting (ResizeImage.net is useful for resizing images).

Below are some free resources which provide creative templates and design ideas for social media posts and stories:-

> Canva.com for posters

> Crello.com for stories. On the website, there is a demo video that will get you started.

- **Facebook and Instagram**

Facebook.com and Instagram.com are two of the most popular social media sites. They both are quite similar, so we decided to talk about them in the same sub-section. Instagram tends to have a greater number of young users (teenagers and people in their 20s and 30s), however recently Instagram has a growing number of older users.

Useful tip: You can use the Instagram and Facebook app in your preferred language. Go to Instagram>Settings> Account and choose your language. For Facebook follow these steps Facebook>Settings>Privacy and choose your language.

To get started follow these steps:-

1. Create a business account

First, download the application on your mobile or visit their website to create an account (business.facebook.com/ createand select "Create Account". Instagram gives you the option to create a business account when you create a new one). If you have an existing account you can always change it to a business account. Business accounts are useful for tracking the activity on your social media page and the data can prove to be useful for understanding your consumers. Once you have a large following on your account, you can calculate statistics such as the average age group of your consumers, what they like and dislike (number of likes on a post) and you can also look at what your competitors are posting.

Useful tips: To increase your follower count, request to follow as many people as you can, so that more people are likely to follow your business back. Also, include a small description of your business in the "bio" section of your profile. Keep your account public!

2. Start Posting

It is important to regularly update your social media pages with information about your business. Remember it is the fastest way to communicate with your customers. Posts could be about anything from new sales or new products to contact information or new store openings.

Instagram and Facebook have two types of postings, a story (disappears in 24 hours) and a post (permanent on your page until you delete it). Some key points to remember while posting are:-

> Use simple language and bright colours to catch people's attention (canva.comand crello.comare good resources to use for this)

> Try not to put too much information on one poster, because it will make it harder to read.

> While posting use hashtags. For example, #diwali #festivalshopping if you are selling diyas. This will increase post visibility (more people are likely to see your post). Use specific hashtags, but make sure they aren't too long because they will be harder to find.

> Include location hashtags such as #bangalore in case you are a local business.

> Post exciting and colourful content regularly (once or twice a day is good) but not too often because this will create spam and people will unfollow.

> More than two billion people use Facebook every month – so no matter what kind of audience you want to reach, you'll find them here.

> Tag people (and brands) on your posts. Tagging your loyal customers or even neighbouring companies and vendors on social media can broaden the reach of your business to new potential customers and will help grow your following. You should also encourage your followers to tag your social media handle or business location in their posts. This will also improve customer loyalty.

3. Direct Messages and Comments

Direct Messages and Comments are two of the simplest ways to interact with your customers. The direct messages features can be used to talk to your customers and answer any questions they might have. Comments are useful for customer feedback and learning about their interests and reactions to specific posts (you can also reply to them).

Useful tip: you can translate Instagram and Facebook comments to your preferred language.

4. Shopping through Social Media Pages

Recently many business owners post pictures of their products on their social media pages along with prices, so if someone is interested in buying their product they can contact the business through the DMs feature or in the comments section. This can prove to be a useful feature if your business is comfortable with delivering products.

Note: <u>Twitter.com</u>is also another popular social media platform, but it does not have as many features. You can post short "tweets" about your business once in a while.

- **Paid Social Media Marketing**

While the above resources are free of cost, social media companies also provide a paid form of advertising. Popular ones include Facebook, Youtube and Instagram. These can be useful for targeted advertising and for larger businesses with bigger marketing budgets (money to spend on advertising).

> <u>business.instagram.com</u>offers step by step instructions on how to promote a post. It is also available in different languages. Just click on "promote post" and then "how to promote post" (can only be done from a mobile phone).

> <u>facebook.com/business</u>> "Create an ad" will also provide a step by step process to create your own page and advert on Facebook. Facebook claims that "if you want to spend Rs. 510 a week, you can. If you want to spend 51 lakhs a week, you can do that too." This site also has valuable information on advertising.

> <u>youtube.com/ads</u>is useful for creating video adverts, in case your product needs to be demonstrated. If you have questions remember to contact their customer service number which is at the top of the webpage. This site gives you specific advice for making a YouTube ad.

> *Useful tip*: if you decide to use paid advertising on social media, always start small to see what you should expect in terms of costs and user interaction.

Social Media Marketing can keep you informed about your target audiences, what they like, and what they don't like. You can use it to get input, answer questions, or listen to any feedback! It provides a variety of opportunities for each and every business – big, small and micro – to attract all kinds of customers, so make use of this channel to its fullest potential.

Chapter 7: Online Deliveries

In today's world, customers want convenience and there is nothing more convenient than having products and services delivered to their homes. Before the COVID-19 pandemic, many microbusiness owners were worried about the setting-up costs and complicated operations that came with online stores; however, with the growing contactless economy (no touch), deliveries have become a necessity for businesses to survive. It is also much easier to keep track of payments and your customers since everything is automatically recorded. In fact, with growing rent and other costs, many business owners have decided to switch to a completely online mode of business. Companies like Amazon and Swiggy have made online deliveries a very simple and cheap process. They even take care of customer service and shipping! Here are a few ways of starting your online sales:-

- **Amazon**

Amazon.in is the first company that comes to mind when you think of online shopping. Amazon is very reliable for deliveries and end to end (start to end) customer care. Amazon may seem like an expensive option but it starts as low as 2 % fee per product and just Rs. 28 for delivery (as of July 2021). Chances are, most of your competing businesses are already selling their products on Amazon, so you should start too before it is too late!

Steps to set up your business on Amazon:-

> Go to sell.amazon.in> click on "start selling"> "create an account" and follow the instructions.

>*Useful tip:* You can use this webpage in your preferred language. To change language, click on the small sign at the top of the webpage that says "English" and choose your language.

- **Courier Services or Dunzo**

Another way to sell online would just be sending images of your products or advertising services through Whatsapp or messages to existing customers and new ones as well. But for this type of service, it is important to first list your business on online directories and marketplaces like IndiaMart (seller.indiamart.com). Then, once customers contact you and place an order, you can ship them the product through courier services like DTDC for a low cost or use the Dunzo app on your mobile (for local pickup and drop services in the same city).

Useful tip: You can also advertise and sell products through your social media pages for your followers to see and place an order. To set up a complete online store and link it to your social media page (see business.instagram.com/shopping or my.ecwid.com)

- **Shopify**

Shopify.com is an easy resource to use to set up a complete online store. It helps you create an online store website for your business and you can list all your products along with product details. It is like your business's very own Amazon! Shopify offers a free trial, but you need to pay to use their services after a few weeks.

- **Swiggy and Zomato**

The Amazon of food deliveries. If you are a local restaurant or grocery store, register to start delivering through Swiggy (download the <u>Swiggy Partner App</u>on your mobile) or go to <u>zomato.com/partner_with_us</u>to register your restaurant (you can also use the <u>Zomato Business App</u>on your mobile).

Online businesses are a cheaper and more convenient way (both for you and your customers) of doing sales. You can also analyze the data from online sales to make the right business decisions. Online deliveries may seem like a huge task at first, but once you get started, you will realise that it has so many benefits!

Useful tip: Remember to add a "thank you" note while delivering your products. This adds a personal touch and helps improve customer satisfaction.

CHAPTER VIII

Section 8: Improving Customer Satisfaction and Business-Specific Tips

In a contactless economy, with decreased face-to-face interactions, it can be hard to communicate with your customers and ensure they are satisfied. But it is important to offer a great customer experience as this will give your business an advantage over the competition and improve brand loyalty (if there are two products A and B in a store, customers will choose your product B only because they like your brand more). Here are some ways to interact with your customers through the online platform:-

- **Feedback Forms**

Ask your customers to fill out simple forms with their thoughts on your products or how they would rate your service. Form links can be shared through email or direct messages on Whatsapp or Instagram.

Useful tip: docs.google.com/forms is an easy way to create forms

- **Social Media platforms**

Most customers want answers immediately and refuse to wait. Social Media platforms are the most useful tools to engage in real-time through comments and direct messages **(see Section 6 Social Media Marketing).**

- **Post-sale communications**

After selling a product or service, contact your customer to ask about their experience. You can always understand what they were expecting, what was good and what was not. The feedback can then be used to improve your product.

- **Reviews and replying**

Always provide an option for your customers to share feedback. This way, not only you, but other customers can also access the reviews. Remember to reply and thank your customers for their feedback.

***

We have also put together some useful resources that will help boost your brand image and increase your customer base. The tips are categorized based on different microbusiness industries. We hope this is helpful as we tried to include the most common types of microbusinesses.

Food and Beverages (F & B) Industry	- Feedback is important. - Send a thank you note along with the food to improve customer relations and add a personal touch - Resource for providing online menu and review- zomato.com/addrestaurant - Ensure health and safety regulations are always met. Hygienic conditions will attract more customers - Extra seasonings and packaging is important during online deliveries! - Social media marketing is big in the food industry. It is all about pictures and visuals. - If you are a grocery store you can deliver groceries to customers by registering on Swiggy (see Section 7 Online Deliveries)

Textile (Cloth) Industry	- Packaging makes all the difference. - Feedback, returns, refunds, customer follow up are very important. - Regularly update your promotions on your social media, it is your most up to date channel. - Do not overproduce or oversupply. Plan out your resources, look at past data on sales. - As a microbusiness it is easy to serve a special segment of your customer base. Target specific needs (where you don't have many competitors) and produce products according to those needs. - You can easily do online sales through social media marketing and other online mediums. Remember to use high quality images!

Health Clinics	- CallADoc(facebook.com/HISAHC360 > click on "send message") is a free, pre symptom checker. - Use Google forms to collect basic information about the patient before consultation. - Practo (practo.com/providers/doctors/profile) is an easy way for patients to book appointments. It is a popular website and you can pay a fee to advertise your clinic on this platform. - HealthCare360 (thehealthcare360.in) will design your online clinic on Facebook. You can always request a demo.

Services (hair salon, mechanics, shoe repair, watch repair, fancy stores, tailoring, tutoring,florists)	- Yellow pages is a great resource for quick and easy online advertising of your products and services (yellowpages.in) - Use regular reliable bills to make invoices; this can make your business more professional. - Listing your employees on platforms like partner.urbancompany.com will help increase their income. - urbanclap.com is great for listing services (use urbanpro.com to list tutoring services)

Other general tips	- Do not take initial negative comments too seriously, every small business faces this. - Maintain records and delete old unnecessary data. - Design invites using greenvelope.com - Use googlemaps.com to add the location of your business so it is easy for customers to find. - Pinterest.com is great for ideas from design to packaging, simply type in the search bar. - Use linkedin to connect with other businesses and improve your brand image. in.linkedin.com - Use Just Dial so that customers can locally search for your businesses and find out about them! For a free listing, just go to (justdial.com/Free-Listing) and provide all the necessary details of your business. - Use VistaPrint (vistaprint.in) to print customized covers and other items with your business logo/name. This improves your business's brand image. - Google has a series of videos to help small businesses like yours. Go to Youtube.com and type "quick help videos google india".

Section 9: Government Schemes for Microbusinesses

1. MSME Business Loans in 59 Minutes
> Provides financial assistance
> Loans under this scheme can extend up to 5 crores
> Loans can take between 8 and 12 days to process
> Approval for the loan can be obtained in 59 minutes
> The rate of interest depends on the type of business
> The interest of loans can begin at 8.5%

ICICI Bank	Punjab and Sind Bank	Yes Bank
Federal Bank	Kotak Bank	Union Bank
Central Bank of India	Indian Bank	UCO Bank
Canara Bank	Indian Overseas Bank	SIDBI
Bank of Maharashtra	IndusInd Bank	SBI
Bank of India	IDFC Bank	Punjab National Bank
Bank of Baroda	IDBI Bank	Saraswat Bank

List of banks that support "MSME Business Loans in 59 Minutes"

2. MUDRA Loans
> Provides money to units of microbusinesses
> For this type of a loan, there are no processing charges and no collateral (an asset or property which the bank can take away in case the borrower cannot pay back the loan -

it is a safety net or guarantee for the bank) is required to be eligible for this scheme

> There is no minimum loan amount for MUDRA loans

> All bank branches in India provide MUDRA loans

Category of loans as follows:

LOAN CATEGORY	LOAN AMOUNT
SHISHU LOANS	Up to Rs. 50,000
KISHORE LOANS	50,000 - 5,00,000
TARUN LOANS	5,00,000 - 10,00,000

3. National Small Industries Corporation (NSIC) Subsidy

> Marketing Support Scheme – The scheme supports any business by creating plans and funding the marketing and operations of the business. This is important as the micro businesses must be supported in order for them to grow.

> Credit Support Scheme – The NSIC provides help and resources to get raw materials for marketing and financing with banks.

The benefit of this scheme is that it offers small industries and businesses access to services without paying any costs. The businesses also do not need collateral for getting financial aid under this scheme.

4. Udyogini

> Udyogini, meaning women empowerment, is a scheme that has been initiated for supporting Indian women who want to start a business.

> The maximum loan offered is Rs. 15,00,000.

> The woman must be between the age of 18 years to 55 years and the annual income of the family of the woman must not be above Rs. 15,00,000.

> There is no limit of income for women who are physically challenged or widowed. There is no processing fee required for getting a loan.

> Women have to provide passport-sized photographs, birth certificate, Below Poverty Line Card, Aadhar Card, Caste Certificate, passbook or bank account, ration card and certification of income.

> There are about 88 categories of businesses that are mentioned for which loans can be provided to women.

5. Credit Guarantee Trust Fund for Micro & Small Enterprises (CGTMSE)

> Collateral free loans for small businesses

> Under the CGTMSE scheme, both new and existing micro and small businesses are eligible for a loan with a maximum credit limit of Rs. 2 crores.

> To get approval for loans more than 10L, you need to provide securities in the form of land or other valuable assets

Useful tip: Make sure to have all the documents such as PAN Card, Aadhar Card, Income Tax Returns Form etc. and ask your bank for assistance. To find a list of the documentation required simply type "what documentation is required for" + *Name of the scheme* in Google. If you want more information about other schemes go to msme.gov.in/all-schemes.

CHAPTER X

Section 10: Success Stories

If you are a microbusiness trying to survive these challenging times, we hope these success stories inspire you to continue working towards your goal. It only takes one good opportunity to change your life!

Rajiv Rao - Fresh World

Rajiv Rao started Fresh World, a vegetable company in 2012 and has since served over 80000 customers! Rajiv has used technology to expand and grow his business! The vegetables were grown from local, organic farmers and were distributed through e- rickshaws and e - autos, technologically-operated vehicles. He used an app, so that customers can know beforehand the route of the vendor or where he is at. The vendors reach all the lanes on their route at a fixed time which helps consumers in coming up with a routine. With the help of an SMS, users are notified about the availability and price of the fruits and vegetables on the cart coming to their doorstep. The process of purchasing vegetables and fruits has become very organised for the consumers and vendors by using GPS-equipped carts and an Android app that provides a digital bill for every purchase.The journey that started with just 5 carts and an initial investment of Rs. 40 lakh, has been successful as Fresh World now has 45 carts and has been able to earn a revenue of almost Rs. 6 crores. Rajiv has big plans for the future of Fresh World as he aims to add 100 more carts and begin operations in Delhi within the next couple of years.

The Weekend Florist - Rachel Chua

"Before you spread yourself too thin, don't be afraid to ask for help. Delegate or outsource tasks that can be done by someone else who might actually be better at it than you." Rachel started working as a florist to release stress and she did it as a hobby initially. She worked part time on the weekends to style weddings and other small events. She took a risk or as she calls it "a leap" when she decided to do this job full-time. Although she found learning everything from scratch to be challenging, she says she is glad to have done it that way. She took a year to build up her website as she was doing everything by herself. "I was the marketer, the salesperson, the bookkeeper, the photographer. I was also the administrator, the delivery woman and of course the florist." She soon decided to launch her website, take on more projects, conduct workshops and achieve more than what she had planned for in 2020. She also outsourced some parts of her work such as social media marketing and deliveries to free up precious time that she can now use to develop and grow the business. Most importantly, she says social media marketing and Ecommerce has helped her significantly in scaling the business. "Building my business online was a great way to start as minimal cost outlay was required. I saved on rent (renting a space in an industrial area vs retail space), saved on renovation cost, hiring cost etc."

StudentCircle - Theo

Theo employs himself as a tutor through his own student-tutoring business, StudentCircle, and he puts most of his profits back into the business. When he first started out, he discovered the world of the Internet and realised that he could use it to do many things, including making his business as popular as it can be. "I found a challenge on the internet. It told me to take an idea I was sure would work and put it on Craigslist (American website that does free online advertising for your business) to see if anyone was actually interested." He has grown his business through customers and how he has interacted with them. He conducted a lot of research to find good-quality tutors. Though he found online advertising to be a little challenging, he says he wouldn't do it any other way. He now employs over 45 people! His number 1 advice for small business owners like you is that you don't need to be big or have a lot of money to grow your business. You must be realistic with your goals and start small but steadily. He also advises growing your savings account -- start saving up so you can take some valuable risks later! "With some money in the bank, you'll have the flexibility to make some moves."

Ching's Secret

Ching's Secret offers a range of Desi Chinese products such as instant Hakka noodles and other sauces. Although the brand did not have any huge competition, it needed to conduct campaigns to gain more popularity. Soon after, Ching's Secret realized that while other mainstream brands marketed themselves heavily on TV, radio, and newspapers, it decided to take a different route on Facebook to launch its first-ever fan page. Thus, Ching's Secret took community building online and went onto becoming India's first branded community with 100K fans. The brand started its journey on the platform in the year 2013 onwards providing a mix of content on Facebook. Ching's Secret cookery channel named 'Ching's Khao Baki Bhool Jaao' was launched on YouTube and Facebook ads were used to reach the exact audience with targeted advertisements. It is now considered one of the most successful Indian case studies on Social Media.

Tamilnadu Auto-Driver Samon's Website: Tuk-Tastik.com

Samson, an auto driver in Chennai, has set up his own website to get national and international customers and build strong brand popularity. My name is Samson and I am an Auto-Rickshaw driver here in Chennai, formally known as Madras. You can find me outside of the Taj Coromandel Hotel in the heart of the city," the website owner says on the Home Page of Tuk-Tastic.com. Besides giving information on himself, Samson has put together a website containing all the information that a tourist would need, under sections such as Eating and Drinking, Shopping, and Days Out. The interactive website allows 'Happy Customers' to share their testimonials on Samson, post pictures of their ride with him, and lets new customers contact him easily. "I have opted for this mode to be in touch with my regular customers and to expand the clientele. I have found this very advantageous." Samson is also the general secretary of the Good Will Auto Stand Union opposite the Taj Hotel in Chennai. Today, Samson has tourists from all over the world including Japan, Denmark, and USA.

CHAPTER XI

Appendix of Resources

To make all the resources mentioned in this book more accessible, we have prepared a list of every single website/ application that was suggested in each of the sections. Hope you find it helpful to start your digitisation journey.

Section 2: Planning Ahead

> Google Account

> EverNote

> google.com/preferences#languages

Section 3: Finance

> Annapurna Microfinance

> Equitas Microfinance

> kickstarter.com

>razorpay.com/x/current-accounts

> business.paytm.com

> pay.google.com

> quickbooks.intuit.com/in

Section 4: Organising Data

> infogram.com/app

> drive.google.com

> nordpass.com

> meet.google.com

> calendar.google.com

> evernote.com

Section 5: Advertising

> wix.com

> wordpress.com

> Google Business

> mailchimp.com

> google.com/adsense/start
> business.google.com/create
> yellowpages.in

Section 6: Social Media Marketing

> unsplash.com
> pixabay.com
> burst.shopify.com
> resizeImage.net
> canva.com
> crello.com
> facebook.com
> Instagram.com
> twitter.com
> business.facebook.com/create
> business.instagram.com
> facebook.com/business
> youtube.com/ads

Section 7: Online Deliveries

> Amazon.in
> sell.amazon.in
> seller.indiamart.com
> dtdc.in
> dunzo.comOR Dunzo App
> business.instagram.com/shopping
> my.ecwid.com
> Shopify.com
>swiggy.comOR Swiggy Partner App
> zomato.com/partner_with_usOR Zomato Business App

Section 8: Improving Customer Satisfaction and Business-Specific Tips

>docs.google.com/forms
> zomato.com/addrestaurant

> facebook.com/HISACalladoc
> practo.com/providers/doctors/profile
> thehealthcare360.in
> yellowpages.in
> partner.urbancompany.com
> urbanclap.com
> urbanpro.com
> pinterest.com
> greenvelope.com
> googlemaps.com
> in.linkedin.com
> justdial.com/Free-Listing
> vistaprint.in
> Youtube.com > "quick help videos google india"

Section 9: Government Schemes for Microbusinesses

>psbloansin59minutes.com/business-loan
> mudra.org.in
> nsic.co.in
> udyogini.org
> cgtmse.in

About The Authors

Anya Pallamreddy, a twelfth-grade student at The International School Bangalore, is extremely passionate about social entrepreneurship and works hard to give back to her community through small but meaningful ways. Apart from going down the rabbit holes of exciting research in her free time, she is also a competitive swimmer, avid reader, a lover of the outdoors, and an absolute movie buff! She hopes to pursue Economics with a concentration in Finance at university in the future!

Anya Pallamreddy (17)

Vinusha Narapareddy, a rising senior at Phillips Exeter Academy, is a passionate social entrepreneur and creative thinker. She has worked for multiple non-profit causes in the past and is committed to building a career at the cross-section of healthcare, technology, and social enterprise. Her interests are widely varied, and she enjoys reading random facts as a hobby! In her free time, she loves to make cards, watch documentaries about the stars and unwind with badminton. A typical "nerd" with a creative flame, and just the person you would expect to author this guide.

Vinusha Narapareddy (17)